Islam,

Its historical beginnings

By

Franklin W. Jackson

Table of Contents

Introduction   Page 4

Chapter 1, Muhammad   page 6

Chapter 2, The Qur'an   page 28

Chapter 3, The Hadith   page 44

Chapter 4, The Jihad   page 47

Chapter 5, Islam and Women   page 56

Chapter 6, Psychological Profile
          Of Muhammad   page 58

Introduction

Although the modern Muslim movement has done more than enough to earn our undivided attention, most people have not bothered to give the history of Islam even a casual glance. I am shocked and dismayed at the extent of ignorance and misinformation that dominates this all important subject, especially among political leadership. It is not possible for anyone to accurately understand the Muslim society unless and until he knows its historical beginnings, including the man and his sayings that still drive the movement today.

There is a reliable historical record of the 14 centuries of the Muslim religion and their society at our disposal. It is not locked up somewhere without a key. From its beginnings in the Arabian Desert in the sixth century, right up to today, there is an historical record from which we may learn invaluable lessons.[1] There are, of course, differing accounts, as there are with even less controversial historical figures. But in order to lessen the chances of accusations of bias against the prophet, I intentionally chose Muhammad, the messenger of God by Betty Keler, as a significant source, because Keler always chose to view the prophet in the most favorable light. She, in turn, relied most heavily upon the early account of Ibn Ishaq which was written in AD 767.

During all those centuries, the events that comprise the history of Islam were recorded without the

---

[1] Biographies of Muhammad date as early as Ibn Ishaq in 767 and edited by Ibn Hisham in 833, al-Waqidi in 823 and Ibn Sa'd in 845.

fear of offense that currently suppresses so much today. In fact, the Muslims were proud of their astounding accomplishments and displayed no desire to hide them. So, with the historical record there for the taking, we will do just that, right here and right now. Only then will we be able to put today's events into historical perspective and discern the truth from the untruths when motives are voiced or denied.

I am not Jewish or politically motivated. I am an historian who has tried to give you an accurate, though admittedly, condensed account, of what may be the single most pressing issue of our day.

Chapter 1
Muhammad

Muhammad's full name was Abu al-Qasim Muhammad ibn 'Abd Allah ibn 'Abd al-Muttalib ibn Hashim.[2] The Qur'an states that his given name at birth was Ahmad (61:6), which means "more praiseworthy". Muhammad means "praised one".[3] His nick-name is said to have been al-Amin, which means "the trustworthy".

Because it is difficult to translate all of the subtleties of the Arabic alphabet into English, there are several spellings of Muhammad's name, including Mohammad, Mohammed and Mahomet. But Muhammad is the most common.[4]

Muhammad was born on August 20, 570 in Mecca (formerly Bekka), Arabia within the tribe of Coreish (Quraysh), which means "sharks", because they made their living from preying on the pilgrims that visited the town. Muhammad's grandfather had discovered a spring nearby that made an interesting sound as it bubbled to the surface. His grandfather decided that this was the very same well that had rescued the famous biblical characters   Hagar and her son Ishmael 2,000 years earlier. (Hagar was maidservant to Abraham's wife

---

2 "ibn" means 'son of'; "abd" means 'servant of'
3 <u>World Book Encyclopedia</u>, World Book, Inc., 2003, Volume 13. "Muhammad", page 910
4 <u>Islam Unveiled</u>, by Robert Spencer, Encounter Books, San Francisco, 2002, at page xiii

Sarah, and Abraham fathered this boy, Ishmael, by her. *Gen. 21:19*) The grandfather's family became caretakers of this "Well Zem-Zem", a name bestowed upon it because of the sound it made, and charged fees from pilgrims eager to drink from this famous well. The clan also had a flourishing business selling protection to caravans passing through the hazardous region. 5

Muhammad's father, Abdullah, was a handsome ladies-man but died at age 25 before Muhammad was born. Immediately after his birth, Muhammad's mother, Amina, gave Muhammad to a Bedouin foster mother[6] to nurse for her, which was not an uncommon practice at that time and place. When the boy was two years old, he was weaned and returned to his mother. But his mother did not want him and persuaded the nurse to keep the boy longer. He stayed with the nurse another two years until a strange thing happened.

One day, little four years old Muhammad announced that, "Two men in white raiment came and threw me down and opened up my belly and searched inside for I don't know what."[7] Many of the local men

---

5 Muhammad, the messenger of God, by Betty Kelen, GRM Associates, Inc., 290 West End Ave., NY, NY, 10023, 1975, at page 6

[6] The first nurse was Thueiba, the slave of Muhammad' uncle Abu Lahab, who nursed Muhammad for only a few days. Nevertheless, Muhammad always retained a devoted reverence for this nurse. The next nurse was Halima.

7 Muhammad, the messenger of God, by Betty Kelen, GRM Associates, Inc., 290 West End Ave., NY, NY, 10023, 1975, at page 9

questioned the boy, but each time he stuck to his story. His foster father said that he had had a stroke. Muslims today usually explain this very odd behavior as a fit. His nurse was most disturbed by this behavior and rushed Muhammad back to his mother and told her the strange story. Again, Amina persuaded the nurse to keep the boy. So off he went again, away from his mother and back to the care of the Bedouin nurse in the tribe Beni Sad.

After one more year, Muhammad had another instance of strange behavior similar to the first. The Bedouin foster mother really liked the boy, however his behavior was just too disturbing to her and her tribe that they insisted that his mother take him back, and for good this time.

Muhammad later said that during these five years with the Bedouins, he learned the pure language of the Arabs.[8]

When Muhammad was 6, his mother took him and their slave[9] on a 200 mile trip through the harsh Arabian Desert to visit her husband's grave in Medina. It was obviously a bad idea, because the conditions were too harsh for Muhammad's mother and she died on the way back[10]. The surviving boy and slave barely made it back to Mecca. He was now an orphan.

---

8 The New Encyclopedia Britannica, 15th Ed., "Muhammad"

[9] Ethiopian slave named Omm Ayman

[10] In Abwa which lies half way between Mecca and Medina

He was taken in by his paternal grandfather, Abd al-Muttalib, where he enjoyed the only good years of his childhood. The grandfather was the revered patriarch of the largest tribe in town and he really liked Muhammad. The boy was allowed to run right up to the great man, while his own sons did not enjoy this privilege. They were required to remain at a respectful distance. But this happy time did not last very long. His grandfather died two years later at age 82. Muhammad grieved terribly over his death and was seen weeping as he walked behind the bier. Muhammad never recovered from this loss. With this loss, Muhammad lost the only good childhood home, the only good role model, and the only security he was ever to know as a child. He left there with a fondness for power and the comforts of life.

Muhammad was then passed on to his uncle Abu Talib.[11] The grandfather's wealth was divided among so many relatives that it left Muhammad's new caretaker a very poor man. As Muhammad says in the Qur'an, he was poor and an orphan (93:6), and grew up in "an uncultivable valley" (14:40).

Although Muhammad was surrounded by a multitude of uncles and cousins his own age, he had no friends and no girlfriend. He was a loner and enjoyed being by himself. Muhammad got into a lot of fights, and somewhere along the way became strongly disliked by the leader of the family clan. During a fight with a boy

---

[11] or Abu Alib

named Abu Jahl, Muhammad kicked Abu in the groin so hard that Abu said he did not just see stars, but he saw "a camel with teeth that did not look like camel's teeth and that tried to eat me."12 We will hear more about Abu Jahl later.

As you might well have imagined, sixth century Arabia was a wild and lawless place, with many fierce tribes constantly at war with one another. All caravans except the largest were sure to be attacked and plundered. The habitable parts of Arabia (now Saudi Arabia) were overcrowded and extremely poor. Mecca was no exception.

When Muhammad was 10 years old, a bloody feud broke out between the two rival clans in Mecca, the Coreish and Beni Hawazin clans, and it lasted for 10 years. It was called the "Wicked Wars" or "Sacrilegious Wars" and all the local men were expected to serve. But Muhammad chose not to fight. He preferred to go to where the enemy's arrows had fallen the thickest on the ground, calmly gather them up and deliver them to his uncle.13 Muhammad earned the reputation as one without courage or martial daring of any kind.

One book describes the young man's appearance:
> "He was of medium height, rather stocky, with a round head set on a very straight spine. He had a headlong way

---

12 Jihad in the West, by Paul Fregosi, Prometheus Books, 1998, 59 John Glenn Drive, Amherst, NY 14228, at pg. 38
13 Muhammad, messenger of God, ibid, page 11

of walking as if he were always going downhill. His complexion was very fair for a member of a sun-blistered race, his hair and beard very black and extremely well tended, the locks falling smoothly over his shoulders. His eyebrows across his nose. He was fussy about his clothes, which were always spotless. His teeth are oddly described-set wide apart in the jaw and pointed like the teeth of a saw."[14]

He is also described as quiet, more likely to listen than speak, modest, mannerly, contemplative, pensive, retiring and very shy with girls. But he was also known to be vindictive and with an unrelenting hatred toward his enemies. He passed through his entire youth without a single notable exploit and without impressing anyone around him to any degree.

---

[14] Muhammad the Messenger of God, by Betty Kelen, Thomas Nelson Inc. Publishers, 1975, pages 33-34

Kelen admits, "He grew up as a boy of no account, and even much later, when all Arabia was talking about him, no one came forward with impressive recollections of his childhood in Mecca."[15]

During an important clan meeting during which the leaders made an oath to protect the oppressed, Muhammad did not participate.

Mecca, by anyone's standards, was a desolate place, and it was almost all Arabic. But each year, there was an annual fair at Ocatz where every sort of person could be seen. Muhammad's uncle took Muhammad there, and it was there that he first encountered other ethnic peoples and religions. Most notably, he met and heard Christians and Jews, sometimes in the form of sermons or lectures. The Arabs called them the "People of the Book". He showed a keen interest and was profoundly impressed with the differences between his culture and theirs and the superior lifestyle enjoyed by the other half. It is impossible to exaggerate the impact that this fair had on his thoughts and ideas and the making of this man.[16] Unfortunately, the Christianity that Muhammad observed had a great deal to be desired.

He also encountered flagrant and fierce prejudice, both ethnic and religious. The Christians and Jews despised the Arabs. The vast majority of Arabs were pagans who worshiped hundreds of gods and practiced

15 ibid, pg. 10
16 Life of Mohomet, Sir William Muir, KCSI, Smith, Elder & Co., 1894

polygamy on a grand scale. The Christians and Jews considered them dirty and uncivilized pagans. This prejudice did not escape Muhammad's attention, and he deeply resented and hated the Christians and Jews for it. But he envied their lifestyle, which was conspicuously better than the Arabs'. He knew that the "People of the Book" worshiped only one God and he thought it was ridiculous that Arabs worshiped hundreds of idols. Muhammad said, "All idols and formulas are nothing but miserable bits of wood. There is only one God."17

Muhammad obviously picked up some of the basic points of Judaism, but in each of his many references to them in the Qur'an, he gets something wrong. Even authors that revere the prophet admit, "scholars want to know where Muhammad learned his rather eccentric Biblical lore."18 He knew that Abraham was beloved of God and was considered the father of faith. He knew that Abraham had two sons and that it was his son Isaac who had inherited the promises of God and was a Patriarch of the Jewish faith. He knew that it was Abraham's other son Ishmael who was the Patriarch of the Arab people. Muhammad was a fiercely patriotic Arab and, as you know, his family cared for the famous well that they believed was the one that had saved Ishmael's life. He naturally revered Ishmael above Isaac

---

17 Jihad in the West, ibid, pg. 34

18 Muhammad the Messenger of God, by Betty Kelen, Thomas Nelson Inc. Publishers, 1975, page27

and would later ride this wave to personal glory. He also saw how self destructive it was for the local chieftains to be constantly at war with each other. He thought the Arabs needed an identity like the Christians and Jews and that the Arabs needed to be united. He tried to gather a following behind his ideas, but because of the bitter tribal rivalries, he was not able to attract any followers, not even from his own Coreish clan. It would appear that this failure was a significant frustration to him, and a cause that he would continue to pursue.

When Muhammad was 25, his uncle explained to him that his desperate finances required that Muhammad live somewhere else, and asked Muhammad to move out. He arranged for Muhammad to work for a rich widow named Khadijah as a camel driver. In exchange for Muhammad, the uncle received four camels.

Khadijah was 15 years older than Muhammad but fell for him almost immediately.[19] She sent someone to ask him how he felt about marrying her and Muhammad agreed. Muhammad had a very good marriage, was always faithful and his wife adored him. They had six children, five of whom died. From this marriage, only Fatima survived him.

Fatima married Ali, the son of Muhammad's Uncle Abu Talib, and all of her descendants are called the

---

19 There is an obvious question about her true age, because if she was 55 when they married as most accounts state, then how could she have borne him six children?

"Fatimid dynasty" and are honored above the rest.[20]

Mecca was home to a religious relic, a black stone about 6" x 8" that attracted many pilgrims. When Muhammad was 35, there was a flood that destroyed the building that housed this stone and it became necessary to rebuild it. When it was time to put the stone into its new resting place, a quarrel broke out among the leading men as to who would have the honor of placing the stone back inside the building. It was decided that the next person to enter the square would decide. Just then Muhammad entered the square and he was presented with the problem. Muhammad removed his mantle, placed the stone on it and told each of the leaders to pick up a corner. He then moved the stone the final distance and all were happy. From this incident, Muhammad saw clearly that there was no decision making authority in the whole Coreish clan, and from then on viewed himself as the chosen leader and judge of his people.

Muhammad, the man and his beliefs

He was a true loner, unusually observant and a real thinker. He had the uncanny ability to look at the Arabs' way of life from the outside and with a critical point of view. From this frame of mind and from the viewpoint of an impoverished orphan, he developed a laundry list of reforms that he proposed. He was outraged at their treatment of orphans who lacked the protection of a clan. He was outraged at the custom of killing newborn girls, who were traditionally buried alive

---

20 World Book Encyclopedia, World Book, Inc., 2003, Volume 13. "Muhammad", page 910

at birth. Because he grew up poor, he was outraged at the Arabs' money grubbing attitude and how they routinely swindled the pilgrims who were their bread and butter. He marveled that Arabs could worship a common stone one day and the next day line their campfire with it.

The second great influence on his life came from the People of the Book. They had an enormous effect upon him. He soaked in their teachings, but rather than convert to either of their religions, he decided to steal their teachings for the Arabs. He was too much of an Arab to be a part of any group that despised Arabs the way the Christians and Jews despised the filthy and pagan Arabs, so he took their teachings for the Arab people. Muhammad invented the idea of an Arab 'People of the Book'. He took some of their biblical beliefs and mixed it with his own social agenda to form a uniquely Arab blend.

Then, he added a touch of brilliance by replacing Isaac with Ishmael, and thereby replacing the Jews and Christians as God's chosen people with the Arabs. So, Ishmael's seed were now God's chosen people. It was pure genius. The scum of the earth were now the most revered people on earth.

He developed a list of things that the Arabs needed to change in order to bring them into the civilized world, and he believed them very strongly:

1. There is no God but God
2. It was a big mistake for Arabs to believe that God did not notice their corrupt ways or care about what they did. In other words, they were accountable.
3. Their money grubbing was wrong

4. Cheating orphans was wrong
5. Swindling pilgrims was wrong
6. Burying baby girls was wrong
7. Worshipping stones was stupid
8. Ishmael was the true heir of Abraham and thus the Arabs were the real chosen people. [21]
    It is extremely important to note that he formed all these personal beliefs before his call as prophet.

The Birth of Islam

    It was in the year 610 that Muhammad announced that the Archangel Gabriel appeared to him in a cave at the foot of Mt. Hira just north of Mecca. It is widely believed that his call is recorded in the Qur'an at 96:1-5: "READ". To which Muhammad said, "I can't read." Gabriel said again, "READ. Recite in the name of your Lord who created, created man from clots of blood. Recite: Your Lord is the Most Beautiful One, who by the pen taught man what he did not know." Later, Gabriel would say, "Oh Muhammad, thou art the Prophet of the Lord in truth and I am Gabriel."[22] What is clear is that Muhammad concluded that he had been chosen as the one true Prophet of God and he had been given unrestricted license by God to start a new religion. It is noteworthy that there are no tenets of faith included in

---

21 <u>Islam Unveiled</u>, by Robert Spencer, Encounter Books, San Francisco, 2002

22 <u>Jihad in the West</u>, ibid, pg. 35

the words of Gabriel's call, and Muhammad would not hear from Gabriel again for at least two years. Nevertheless, Muhammad immediately began to preach his gospel of social change. His preaching consisted of those same points that we have already covered. He also warned that God was watching man's behavior and will judge him for it. In the Arab culture of that time, all of this was very new and different. But now the message was very different than before. Now he had been anointed by an angel of God to be God's messenger with the message.

In Muhammad's new religion, he named god 'Allah', which was the name of their current supreme Semitic deity. As already stated, he also replaced Isaac, the father of the Jews, with Ishmael, the father of the Arabs, so God's promises to Abraham now belonged to the Arabs instead of the Jews and God's chosen people were now the Arabs instead of the Jews. But now, his words were being recorded, so it was all repeated for the Qur'an.[23] It was pure genius and would prove to be a very enticing prospect to many an Arab.

Muhammad explained that the Jews needed to be replaced because they were guilty of all kinds of evil. He said they were greedy[24], slew the prophets[25], charged

---

[23] Qur'an 2:125-143, 4:163, 19:54-55, 21:85-86,

[24] Qur'an 2:96, 62:6-8

[25] Qur'an 2:87, 91; 3:21, 181; 4:155, 5:70

usury[26], did not believe, were blasphemous[27], and worked iniquity[28]. Because of this shameful behavior, the Jews had squandered their inheritance and made it necessary for God to turn to Abraham's other son, Ishmael.

His wife Khadijah was his first convert and then his two adopted sons Ali and Zeid, who was Black. Then a few local friends joined him. All the early followers joined out of personal loyalty to Muhammad. It was pivotal when Abu Bakr, a rich merchant, became a disciple.[29] Suddenly, Muhammad had a major backer and instant legitimacy. Likewise, his fiercest opposition came from personal enemies, like from the chief of his own clan, Abu Sufyan, who hated his guts, and also from the man that Muhammad had kicked in the groin, Abu Jahl.

After Muhammad claimed to be God's prophet, it was open warfare between Muhammad and his enemies, mainly Abu Jahl and the other merchants in Mecca who stood so much to lose if their corrupt ways were curtailed by this reformer. Muhammad sent out armed bands to attack his enemies' caravans and vice-versa.

---

[26] 4:161

[27] 5:41, 64; 59:2, 11

[28] 5:41-42, 78-81; 59:2-4, 11-17

29 World Book Encyclopedia, World Book, Inc., 2003, Volume 13. "Muhammad", page 911

Muhammad claimed for himself one-fifth of the money and slaves stolen in these raids. This was to become the right of all "caliphs" who would succeed him as the spiritual and military leaders of Islam.

The conflict was primarily fueled by financial interests. Meccans acquired considerable income from pilgrims coming to see the black stone and Muhammad's new religion posed a serious threat to their tourist industry. The conflict reached a critical stage and Muhammad was forced to compromise. He agreed that three of the pagan idols were indeed valid and that his followers could face Jerusalem when they prayed.

In 619, both his wife Khadijah and his uncle died. This abrupt decline in fortunes in Mecca, together with an invitation from leading citizens of Medina to come share his new religion with them, prompted a gradual move to Medina, a city 350 km northeast of Mecca. Although this left his rival tribe in complete control of Mecca, the animosity only intensified and there were many fierce battles between the Meccans and Muhammad. During one battle, Muhammad captured his old enemy Abu Jahl. Muhammad had him beheaded and his head thrown at Muhammad's feet.

Muhammad did not tolerate any criticism, and during this time of struggle to establish his power, a local woman, Asma bint Marwan, wrote a disparaging poem about him. Muhammad had her killed. Her assassin stabbed her so hard that she was pinned to the couch. Another local poet, Abu Afak, was likewise killed for writing critically of Muhammad, even though he was 100 years old. Another poet had his throat cut just because Muhammad heard that he had met with one of Muhammad's enemies.

To better understand this threat, we must understand the important place poetry played in an Arab's life. Poetry was the closest thing to culture in the bleak Arabian's life. There were no books, so telling stories was very popular and poetry was used to liven up those stories. It was the favored means of communication and the best way to be remembered or worse way to be slandered. Even normal conversation had to be colorfully enhanced by poetic style for it to be that of a true Arab. For instance, it was much better to say, "Oh Lord of a thousand fleas" than "You dirty bum." The poetry was always about one of only six subjects, such as the charms of his mistress, his tribe, or his camel, and was never so blessed as to have any story or plot. Their poetry was also full of the traditional Arab vices: vainglory, envy, vindictiveness and pride. So when Muhammad felt the sting of a poet, he just had him or her killed.

The war between Muhammad and the Meccans ended in 627 with the Battle of the Trench, during which Muhammad dug a huge trench around Medina to defend against a Meccan army of 10,000. After this great victory, Muhammad's control of the area was complete and he was now securely established as a true power in Arabia.

It was at this point in his life that Muhammad's entire approach to leadership changed. Up until now, he preached social reform. He had been a bold moral crusader and it was this battle cry that had propelled him to leadership and power. After the Battle of the Trench, the social reformer was replaced by a military commander with absolute authority and a religious prophet whose every word was from God Himself. From now on, most of the messages that he would receive from Gabriel related to his apostolic authority and personal desires.

Military command is one of the most powerful seductresses that a man can face. And if you add untold riches and an endless supply of beautiful young women, then even the noblest social agenda will not be able to compete.

There were three Jewish tribes in Medina when Muhammad arrived. Although they had financed his stay in town up to this point, Muhammad no longer needed them and he had noticed that they had all the money and the best property.

Muhammad heard that a Jew named Kinana had a fortune in gold hidden somewhere, so Muhammad had him tortured until he gave up the secret. Nevertheless, he was beheaded. Then Muhammad took not only the man's treasure, but also his wife Safiya to be one of his wives.

One day at the marketplace, a Jewish boy raised the skirt of an Arab girl. The boy was promptly killed and Muhammad ordered the entire Jewish tribe out of town. They could leave with their lives if they left all their possessions with Muhammad. They did. Then he ordered the second Jewish tribe to leave, ...without their wealth. They did. Now, there was only one Jewish tribe left in Medina, the Banu Qurayza (Qurayzah). What Muhammad did to them is the stuff of legend. Muhammad had all the men and boys, and possibly one woman, killed. The given number of people killed ranges somewhere between 600 and 800. They were all brought into the town marketplace and beheaded, one at a time, in front of Muhammad. The massacre lasted from morning until well into the night. He watched with relish as head after Jewish head was severed in front of him. He left the spectacle only long enough to enjoy the pleasures of a particularly pretty Jewish girl, whose husband Muhammad had just beheaded. Her name was Reihana.

This incident is of enormous concern to the portion of the Muslim world that claims that theirs is a religion of peace. If the reader were to conduct an internet search of "Massacre of Banu Qurayza", he would find plenty of accounts and commentaries that review the incident is extravagant detail; some voicing outrage and others offering explanations.

Nevertheless, after all were dead, it was time for Muhammad to count the plunder:

over 1,000 women and children sold into slavery
1,500 swords and scimitars
1,500 shields
1,000 spears

300 coats of mail
all their livestock (camels, goats, sheep and horses)
all their land and houses
all their money and jewelry

And pursuant to Muhammad's law, one-fifth went to him.

To quash any criticism of his actions, Muhammad announced that Gabriel had bestowed his blessing on the massacre and Muhammad's good fortune (Sura 33, verses 25-27), and also warns his wives not to object to his affairs. (33:32-35)

Flushed with victory, Muhammad announced that his followers must now face Mecca, his birthplace, when they prayed, instead of Jerusalem.

Muhammad never expressed or showed any remorse after any assassination or execution. Rather, he rejoiced piously with his assassin, promising the killer great rewards in heaven for his deed. Once after the assassin threw a head at Muhammad's feet, Muhammad rewarded him with his walking stick. Another time when the assassin came back to report that the deed had been done, he asked the great Prophet if he had any regrets about what they had just done. Muhammad answered, "None. A couple of goats will hardly knock their heads together."[30] Another time after an enemy's head was rolled in front of him, Muhammad said that he would rather have that head than the best camel in Arabia.

---

30 Jihad in the West, ibid, pg. 47

Muhammad loved war. During his 10 years in Medina, he conducted an amazing 65 military campaigns, or razzias. He also loved the power, money and women that came to him after each successful military campaign. The same was true for his warriors. These men, who not long ago had been poor, miserable desert tribesmen at the bottom of the world's heap, were suddenly rich and powerful men to be feared. They were also part of an exciting adventure. They were soldiers in God's army whose job it was to kill all the people they hated, steal all their money and keep all their beautiful teenage girls to be their sex slaves, or, if they preferred, sell them. What could possibly be better than that? Their wildest dreams had come true. Each hot blooded young warrior was instructed by the man who was both the warrior's spiritual leader and military commander that it was God's will that he have beautiful young women as his sex slaves to do for him whatever he wanted, whenever he wanted it. And they took up this offer with religious zeal.

From his base in Median, Muhammad conquered most of the Arabian Peninsula. The greatest and last of his major campaigns was at the end of the year 630 when he took an army of 30,000 warriors to invade and conquer Syria.

His last battle was in Mutah, Jordan, for the express purpose of acquiring the beautiful and very sharp Mashrafujah swords. Much of the world was about to find out just how sharp they really were.

In June of the year 632, Muhammad suddenly fell

ill, complained of a headache and died at the age of 62. He was buried in Medina.

Without a doubt, Muhammad convinced many of his divine calling and inspired them to zealously follow his vision to conquer the world in his name. There have been many men in history who have tried to recruit an army of devoted followers to fulfill their dreams of conquest who cannot claim the same success that Muhammad can.

Muhammad *was* the right man, with the right message, for the right people, at the right time, if your only criterion is success, because without a doubt, he had great success.

***

You now know more accurate information about Muhammad than 99% of the world's population, including Muslims.

Today in the Muslim world, the disparity between the true historical Muhammad and the Muhammad revered by Muslims is absolutely enormous. This point is repeatedly made by Paul Fregosi in his wonderful book The Jihad in the West, where he quotes historian Malise Ruthven: "The Muhammad who is lodged in the Muslim psyche is not the same as the Muhammad of history."[31] (I strongly recommend this book.)

---

[31] at page 38

Chapter 2
The Qur'an

Muhammad could neither read nor write and there was no paper around for those who could. Every word of the Qur'an was dictated by Muhammad to a scribe who literally scratched it onto a leaf, stone or bone. This heap of "records" was piled in a corner of his tent. There was no order to their storage in a chronological sense. This fact comes across very clearly to any reader of the Qur'an, even though early editors devotedly tried to arrange the thousands of verses in some sensible order. Today's Qur'an is separated into topical sections.

The story of how the Qur'an was canonized is a vast array of conflicting accounts and questionable practices. The collection of the verses was done with such religious zeal that the searchers pursued any source, no matter how tenuous. The results are highly suspect and have been constantly challenged and criticized.

The first two caliphs who succeeded Muhammad were unconcerned about a written text until the battle of Yamana in 633 when 700 warriors who had memorized the Qur'an were killed, including Sālim, the man entrusted by Muhammad to teach the Qur'an. This prompted the caliph Abu Bakr to commission Muhammad's principal scribe, Zaid, to collect the "records" for a written record. Zaid replied, *"By Allah, if he (Abu Bakr) had ordered me to shift one of the mountains it would not have been harder for me than what he had ordered me concerning the collection of the Qur'an... So I started locating the Qur'anic material and collecting it from parchments, scapula, leafstalks of date palms and from the memories of men."* [32]

Once the idea of recording his sayings was conceived, it caught on and numerous versions of the Qur'an passed throughout the Muslim world. This prompted the third caliph, Uthman (644-655), to truly canonize the record. He collected dozens of versions, chose one, burned all the rest and declared his choice the chosen and pure version. Nevertheless, no fewer than 7, and as many as 14, different versions of the Qur'an persisted for many years. It is undisputed that a large portion of today's Qur'an is founded up nothing more than oral tradition.

The initial problem that I had with the Qur'an was making any sense out of many of the verses. The publisher/translator's introduction to most editions of the Qur'an extol the significance of the book and brilliance of its author, yet feel compelled to also include numerous explanations and excuses for the author's incoherence and confusing style. It is generously characterized as "elliptical and allusive". [33]

Now I will ask the reader to bear with me as I share my personal opinions about the Qur'an, and for good reason. I have yet to meet a single non-Muslim who

32 The Qur'an, a user's guide, by Farid Esack, at pg. 86
33 Muslims, their religious beliefs and practices, by Andrew Rippin, 1990, Routledge, 270 Madison Ave., NY, NY 10016, page 45

has actually read it, so I took it upon myself to do so and fill this vast void in the Western World's education. So, here goes:

For me, it was like a wrestling match, with me trying to pin the author down as to what exactly he was trying to say. Many times, the reader cannot tell who is talking, whom he is talking to, and, most of the time, what he is talking about. To this reader, the Qur'an was just a lot of rambling thoughts. It reminded me of my college days when we stayed up late at night and expounded profoundly upon all aspects of life. Mohammed certainly had a lot of opinions on a lot of topics, but don't we all? If that was the way Gabriel spoke, then Gabriel had a very disorganized thought process, very poor literary skills, and very undeveloped powers of reasoning and persuasion. The most outrageous and revolutionary ideas are stated in a matter of fact manner. There is no attempt to support the ideas with new information or reasoning or any attempt to argue the point, no matter how contrary it is from traditional ideas of marriage, war, life or death. On the whole, for me it was an excruciating labor to struggle through this endless stream of disorganized gibberish. No matter which religion one might choose, I think it should go without saying that God, whoever he might be, is more intelligent, wise, knowledgeable, discerning, foresighted, literate and organized than any man. Not a single one of those characteristics of God's presumed nature is remotely evident in this book.

My grandfather used to say, "There's many a slip between the cup and the lip." If the mighty Archangel Gabriel spoke anything at all to Muhammad, there was apparently many a slip between Gabriel's cup and Muhammad's lips.

I am not alone in my frustration with the book.

"The text of the Qur'an presents many ambiguities, difficult words whose precise readings are uncertain, problems of textural division, and apparently incompatible statements."[34]

and

"...an important point about the composition of the book itself--its apparent random character and seeming arbitrary sense of organization"[35]

and

"The literary state of the Qur'an is used against the Muslims by al-Kindi as proof of its non-divine origin."[36]

In fact, the first task of the Muslims themselves in the early days was to make some sense out of the book.

"They appear to have been more concerned with cataloguing the peculiarities of the text itself and facing the practical job of understanding the text, rather than worrying about defending its intricacies."[37]

In addition to making some sense of it, there was

---

34 <u>Muslims, Their religious beliefs and practices</u>, Andrew Rippin, Routledge, 1990, pag. 40
35 ibid, pg. 33
36 ibid, pg. 39
37 ibid, pg. 40

the matter of defending it, for it came under immediate attack for its glaring and multiple problems. In the year 830, the scholar al-Kindi wrote:

"Show me any proof or sign of a wonderful work done by your master Muhammad, to certify his mission, and to prove what he did in slaughter and rapine was, like the other, by Divine command."[38]

and

"...in your book *(Qur'an)*, histories are all jumbled together and intermingled; an evidence that many different hands have been at work therein, and caused discrepancies, adding or cutting out whatever they liked or disliked. Are such, now, the conditions of a revelation sent down from heaven?"[39]

I started reading it with the expectation that it would contain at least some small degree of divine or supernatural "spark". It does not. There is nothing in it that reveals any new revelation about God; nothing at all about His nature or what He is like. There wasn't a single thing that Gabriel told Muhammad that wasn't within the easy reach of human imagination. Nothing he said had the unmistakable label of divine inspiration. I was most keenly aware that the writing is limited to a very human level, or to be more accurate, a very carnal level. It is one man's ranting. His attitude is the most conspicuous feature. He is bitter, more bitter and most

---

38 ibid, pg. 38
39 ibid, pg. 39

bitter.

It sounds a lot more like what would pop into the head of an uneducated Arab who just ducked into his tent to think up a quick answer to the problem of the moment than it sounds like the genius of the God who designed the creation. It is phrased in language that is more like the language of an uneducated camel driver than the language of the God whose prose renders mere mortals speechless. It is also set forth with the bluntness of an autocrat who felt no need to, or lacked the capacity to, offer the reasoning and justification for radical new ideas that contradict the most firmly held convictions of the known world. Such an oversight would not have slipped by the Archangel Gabriel unnoticed.

In the Qur'an, Muhammad makes short work of the Christian faith by brushing aside Jesus as a mere human.[40] He also ridicules the belief that God could have a Son:

"they falsely attribute to Him (Allah) sons and daughters without knowledge…How could He have a son when He has no consort, and He, Himself created everything". (6:100-101)

And he disparages the Jews' behavior as sinful in

---

[40] "The Messiah, Jesus son of Mary, was no more than God's apostle and His Word which He cast to Mary: a spirit from Him. So believe in God and His apostles and do not say; 'Three', Forbear, and it shall be better for you. God is but one God. God forbid that He should have a son!" Qur'an 4:171-172

many areas. But the Qur'an does not dispute the revelation of God given to the Jews or the law given to the Moses. He quotes Moses often and repeatedly makes statements that presume the reader's knowledge of the Bible, then goes on to contradict its most basic tenets. This presents Islam with a big problem because the god of the Qur'an has a totally different nature than the God of the Jews, without offering any explanation for the change.

Two thousand years earlier, God had told Moses, "Thou shalt not kill", "Thou shalt not steal", "Thou shalt not commit adultery", "Thou shalt not covet" and "Thou shalt remember the Sabbath and keep it holy"[41], to mention just a few. Nowhere in God's revelation of Himself and His ways to the Jews was there anything about a Jihad of world conquest, a rampant slave trade or the beheading of all infidels.

The inescapable conclusion that any reader of the Qur'an must draw is that God's nature had changed and His ways and laws had changed. It was now not only permissible to kill, steal, commit adultery and behead unbelievers, it was God's command to do so. This is a pretty significant change. But no matter the magnitude of the change or the limitless ramifications it might have, Muhammad announced a total reversal in the nature of God without giving any explanation at all. That is an

---

[41] Bible, Exodus, Chapter 20

oversight of monumental proportions.

Another conspicuous oversight in the Qur'an is the creation of a system without any safeguards against excess. There is no system, order or organization of any kind. There is no accountability built in anywhere. It is a collection of many ideas, but principally it is a call for the conquest of the entire world in the name of Allah and certain restrictions on personal behavior. But it omits any organization or system of controls to safeguard against tyranny or excess. It would appear that Muhammad was not concerned about excess. Muhammad just did not care if this thing that he started might go wildly out of control. He was content to start an engine that might do as much damage as it did. This total lack of concern is more consistent with the man we know than with an all knowing God.

Then there is the little matter of the boyhood enemy that Muhammad kicked in the balls. Surah 23 verses 1 and 6 read, "Successful indeed are the believers... who guard their private parts."

Although it would seem only natural for the Qur'an to receive the same scrutiny as the Bible, it has not been the case. The Bible has been intensely scrutinized for millennia by multitudes of skeptics who have relentlessly searched for any inconsistency or contradiction. To my knowledge, all they have found are things that do not conform to their lifestyles.

On the other hand, the Qur'an has only one author, but is full of inconsistencies, contradictions and gaping holes. In response to these charges, its defenders claim that it is meant to be recited and heard rather than read, and that hearing it is more important than understanding it. Or they say that it must be read in Arabic to achieve true understanding. The Muslim faithful are unconcerned with scrutinizing the Qur'an to the point that they are totally disinterested in any flaws, weaknesses or problems of any kind. Non-Muslim critics are cast aside without the slightest consideration and Muslim critics don't live long enough to say anything twice.

Muhammad dictated the Qur'an to several scribes.[42] One of them, Abdallah ibn-Abi Sarh, inserted slight changes into Muhammad's dictation to see if he would notice. When Muhammad did not, Abdallah doubted the prophet and left him.

A Call to War

I will never forget the impact it made on me when I first read the Qur'an. I thought "This is an all out call to attack, attack, attack." I wondered how anyone could possibly believe any Muslim who claimed that his is a peaceful religion. Such a one certainly did not expect his audience to check out his sources. I easily found 33 passages from the Qur'an that call for a deadly Jihad

---

[42] Ibn Thalbit, Ali b Abi Talib, Khalid b Sa'id, Aban b Sa'id, Zayd Ibn Thabit and Abdallah ibn-Abi Sarh.

against the infidels of this world, and I list them below. (I could have included many more) Give them your normal interpretation, and then ponder the fact that they are taken by Muhammad's followers as divine commands (emphasis added):

"**There is life for you in retaliation.**" (2:179)

"And **kill them** wherever they find them...but if they do fight you, then **slay them**; such is the recompense of the unbelievers." (2:191)

"**Fighting is enjoined to you**" (2:216)

"And **fight** in the way of Allah, and know that Allah is hearing, knowing." (2:244)

"And may it not be that you would not fight if **fighting is ordained for you?**" (2:246)

"**Taste the chastisement of burning.**" (3:181)

"**Fight then in Allah's way**; this not imposed on you except in relation to yourself, and rouse the believers to ardor, maybe Allah will restrain the fighting of those who disbelieve, and Allah is strongest in prowess and strongest to **give an exemplary punishment.**" (4:84)

"**seize them and kill them wherever you find**

them" (4:89, 4:91)

"Allah shall grant to the strivers above the holders back a mighty reward." (4:95)

"And be not weak hearted in pursuit of the enemy." (4:104)

"The punishment of those who wage war against Allah and His apostle and strive to make mischief in the land is only this, that **they should be murdered or crucified or their hands and their feet should be cut off on opposite sides...**" (5:33)

"And whoever takes Allah and His apostle and those who believe for a guardian, then surely the party of Allah are they that **shall be triumphant.**" (5:56)

"O you who believe! When you meet those who disbelieve marching for war, then turn not your backs to them. And whoever shall turn his back to them on that day, unless he turn aside for the sake of **fighting** or withdraws to a company, then he, indeed, becomes deserving of Allah's wrath, and **his abode is hell; and an evil destination shall it be.**" (8:15-16)

"They rejected the communications of their Lord, therefore **we destroyed them on account of their faults** and we drowned Firon's people, and they were all unjust.

Surely the vilest of animals in Allah's sight are those who disbelieve, then they would not believe." (8:54-55)

"And **prepare against them what force you can** and horses tied at the frontier, to frighten thereby the enemy of Allah and your enemy and others besides them, whom you do not know (but) Allah knows them; and whatever thing you will spend in Allah's way, **it will be paid back to you fully** and you shall not be dealt with unjustly." (8:60)

"O Prophet! **Urge the believers to war.**" (8:65)

"So when the sacred months have passed away, **then slay the idolaters wherever you find them, and take them captives and besiege them and lie in wait for them in every ambush...Allah is Forgiving, Merciful.**" (9:5)

"**Fight the leaders of unbelief**" (9:12)

"**Fight them; Allah will punish them by your hands and bring then to disgrace**, and assist you against them and heal the hearts of a believing people." (9:14)

"**Fight those who do not believe in Allah**, nor in the latter day, nor do they prohibit what Allah and His apostle have prohibited, **nor follow the religion of truth, out of those who have been given the Book, until they**

pay the tax in acknowledgment of superiority and they are in a state of subjection." (9:29)

"O you who believe! What (excuse) have you that when it is said to you: Go forth in Allah's way, you should incline heavily to earth; are you contented with this world's life instead of the hereafter? But the provision of this world's life compared with the hereafter is but little. **If you do not go forth, He will chastise you with a painful chastisement."** (9:38-39)

"Go forth light and heavy, and **strive hard** in Allah's way with your property and your persons." (9:41)

"O prophet! **Strive hard against the unbelievers** and the hypocrites and **be unyielding to them;** and their abode is hell, and evil is the destination....**Allah will chastise them with a painful chastisement in this world and the hereafter."** (9:73-74)

"Surely Allah has bought of the believers their persons and their property for this, that they shall have the garden; **they fight in Allah's way, so they slay and are slain;** a promise which is binding on Him in the Taurat and the Injeel and the Qur'an; and who is more faithful to his covenant than Allah? Rejoice therefore in the pledge which you have made; and that is the mighty achievement." (9:111)

"And **the Jews say:** Uzair is the son of Allah; and **the Christians say: The Messiah is the son of Allah;** these are the words of their mouths; they imitate the saying of those who disbelieved before; **may Allah destroy them;** how they are turned away."(9:30)

"**you who believe! Fight those of the unbelievers who are near to you and let them find in you hardness.**" (9:123)

"**And do not kill anyone whom Allah has forbidden, except for a just cause, and whoever is slain unjustly, we have indeed given to his heir authority, so let him not exceed the just limits in slaying;** surely he is aided." (17:33)

"**So when you meet in battle those who disbelieve, then slice their necks until when you have slaughtered them... as for those who are slain in the way of Allah, He will by no means allow their deeds to perish.**" (47:4)

"**And be not slack so as to cry for peace and you have the upper hand.**" (47:35)

"Say to those of the dwellers of the desert who were left behind: you shall soon be invited (to fight) against a people possessing mighty prowess; **you will fight against them until they submit; then if you obey,**

Allah will grant you a good reward; and if you turn back as you turned back before, He will punish you with a painful punishment." (48:17)

"Surely Allah loves those who fight in His way in ranks as if they were a firm and compact wall." (61:4)

"O Prophet! Strive hard against the unbelievers and the hypocrites, and be hard against them; and their abode is hell; and evil is the resort." (66:9)

***

Whatever the source, inspiration or quality of the Qur'an, and whatever present day Muslims may say about the book today, it is a historical fact that Muslims in the past took the Qur'an as God's command to kill and conquer every non-Muslim person on earth, to decapitate the defeated army, to rape all the women, abduct all the beautiful young girls to serve them as sex slaves, sell the marketable population into slavery, decapitate the professing Christians and Jews and then subject the occupied country to an occupation so ruthless and savage that Hitler's occupation of Europe seems downright civilized. That is an historical fact documented over a dozen centuries.

By the end of the first 110 years, followers of the Qur'an found themselves sitting on top of a huge, rich, powerful and very satisfying empire, achieved at the hands of illiterate desert tribesmen. They couldn't even read. They lacked both the capacity and the desire to question the Qur'an. They were all sitting in such an admirable position that no one was going to question the book behind it all. It was better to revel in their success than tear it all down by undermining the Qur'an. So the empire remained and the Qur'an with it. In their minds, you can't have one without the other and they certainly didn't want to give up what they had. So to this day, the Qur'an remains above question or scrutiny despite the fact that it is so very vulnerable to both.

In more recent times, at the Munich Olympics in 1972, Muslim terrorists murdered Israeli athletes. In 1979, Muslims stormed the US Embassy in Iran and took 52 hostages. In 1983, in Beirut, a Muslim suicide bomber blew up a Marine barracks and killed 241. In 1985, Muslims threw the wheelchair bound Leon Klinghoffer off the cruiseship *Achille Lauro*. In 1993, Muslims bombed the World Trade Center. In 1996, Muslims bombed and killed 19 American soldiers at the Khobar Towers in Saudi Arabia. In 1998, they bombed the US Embassies in Tanzania and Kenya. In 2000, they bombed the USS Cole. And in 2001, on 9-11, they killed over 3,000 at the Twin Towers in NY City. Since then, there have been so many bombings and attacks that they hardly make the news any more. There is one almost every day.

There are numerous Muslim organizations dedicated to the killing of all infidels and the tearing down of the Western culture. Al-Qaeda, Hezbollah, Islamic Jihad, and Hamas are just a few. But, if you have read the Qur'an, then you know that they are really just doing what their Qur'an commands them to do.

Chapter 3
The Hadith

The first 110 years of the Jihad left the Arab world in shock, dismay and euphoria. Millions of destitute desert dwellers had been catapulted to levels of grandeur that most men could only dream about. (I say men, because the women didn't matter) Most had slaves, many had harems and all were rich and ruled a kingdom that stretched half way around the world. And no one was more aware of the change and of the man who had made it all possible than they were. The entire society was fixated on Muhammad. They had the Qur'an, but that says very little about the man. They wanted to know about the man, anything and everything about the man. Just try to imagine how much interest there was in this man at that time. It would be like all the interest in Frank Sinatra in the 1940's, Elvis in the 1950's and the Beatles in the 1960's, all put together. Every Muslim boy grew up wanting to be like him. Every Muslim girl dreamed about what it must have been like to be his wife. All the men vied to be the one most devoted to his teaching. And they all wondered about him. They had heard that he liked honey, hated bad smells, liked the color green and was right handed, but they wanted more.

In response to this insatiable thirst, devout believers set out to dig up every bit of information about him that they could find. Some devoted their entire lives to this holy quest. The problem, of course, was that it had been 110 years. But off they went, in search of books or anybody who knew anything. They found plenty of talkative people and over 600,000 stories about him were uncovered. From the 600,000 stories told, 7,275 were chosen and these comprise the *hadith*, or sacred traditions of Muhammad, which enjoys an authority nearly as great as the Qur'an.

The searchers were particularly eager to find any evidence of a miracle by Muhammad. This is certainly to their credit. After all, if miracles validated the truth of the Jewish and Christian religions shouldn't the greatest and last of all the prophets of God do the same or better? Sadly for them, no credible account of a miracle by Muhammad was uncovered. This was a major disappointment back then, and still is a problem for Islam today. The People of the Book could pull out and put on display a myriad of miracles by their founders. Whenever Old Testament prophets were challenged by the Jews, who were not the least bit timid so to do, God came through for them and put His miraculous stamp of approval on His prophet. Likewise in the New Testament, Jesus and later His apostles were constantly called upon to prove that they really did have a better connection with God than their critics, and readily answered with power on hundreds of occasions. For 21 years, Muhammad fought to convince people that he was God's man. If he had any evidence, he would have provided it, and his devout researchers would have found it. They did not.

During this time in the Muslim world, the best way for a litigant to win a law suit in court was to claim that Muhammad had said something about the contested issue that agreed with his position, because the judge was compelled to do as Muhammad would have done. Those in search of the *hadith* found this practice a major source of questionable traditions.

In the year 772, a man named Ibn Abi al-Awja, who had contributed 4,000 of the traditions that had been considered for the *hadith*, confessed just before his execution in Iraq that he had made them all up. How many were included, no one knows.[43]

It was a very difficult task to narrow 600,000 down to 7,275, and it is reasonable to assume that the criteria employed by these very zealous followers when making their selections was slanted in the prophet's favor.

---

43 <u>Jihad in the West</u>, ibid, pg. 64

Chapter 4
The Jihad

After his death in 632 AD, Muhammad was succeeded by Abu Bakr, who was the father of Aisha, Muhammad's six year old wife. He was the first "caliph", or sole military and spiritual leader, and he served as caliph for two years. He took over a very motivated army at a very opportune time. It was so fortuitous because the closest empires, the Greek Byzantine and Persian Empires, were badly weakened by fighting each other for 250 years. He attacked, but died two years later before seeing the victory. The wars against the Byzantines and Persians lasted from 632 to 640AD. I hesitate to use the word "wars" because the Jihad really was one long war of conquest that lasted over 1,250 years. It would be more accurate to call them battles or campaigns.

The second caliph, Omar, was also Muhammad's father in law. He ruled for 10 years (634-644). Omar made it quite clear that to him it was not about Allah, it was all about the money and women. He was murdered by a Persian slave.

The third caliph was Othman, who had married two of Muhammad's daughters. (Muhammad had 11 wives after Fatima died). He was murdered by the first caliph's son. After that, there were two main rivals for the leadership: the majority Sunnis and the minority Shiites, each side claiming to be the rightful heir to the throne, a rivalry that lives on today. However, at the time, neither was able to grab the leadership, and in the confusion, the son of Abu Sufyan, an old enemy of Muhammad, jumped in and grabbed it. So, Muawiya, the son of Muhammad's worst enemy, ruled the Muslim world and led it to even greater glory.

The Greek Byzantines and Persians were finally defeated and subjected to the usual consequences. The Christians and Jews were decapitated or sold into slavery. All the wealth was confiscated and their countries occupied.

The Muslim army then turned its attention toward the Mediterranean islands of Cyprus, Rhodes and Crete. The savagery inflicted on these innocent infidels may have been normal in the seventh century, but it sure did make this 21st Century reader gag.

From there the Jihad spread in all directions. In the west, it spread from N. Africa up into Spain, which serves as a good example of just how much sex powered the Jihad engine. In the year 711, Spain was ruled by the Visigoths. Their King Don Rodrigo either raped or seduced a teenage Greek girl named Florinda. The girl's father, Count Julian, who lived across the Mediterranean Sea in Morocco, swore vengeance. To that end, Count Julian approached the Muslim ruler of N. Africa, emir Musa, with a proposal to invade Spain. Count Julian pointed out Spain's vulnerable points and the unrest of the native population, but to clinch the deal, the Count promised many pretty young girls for the emir's harem and the warriors' tents. It was a plan for mass abduction and deportation on a truly grand scale.

The Spanish king sat on silk cushions on a tier carried by porters behind an "army" of peasants armed with pitchforks. So Spain joined the other nations that lost their battle. Then they lost all their property and money and then lost all their marketable people, who were either sold into slavery or kept as sex slaves. Spain then endured the longest occupation of any European country, 777 years. But the Spanish never stopped fighting their Moorish conquerors. The entire period of occupation was honored with many brave battles pitched by a Spanish population that never gave up. They fought battle after battle working their way south. The best commander of the 'Spanish Reconquest' was El Cid (11th Century) who is one of the few personalities of the entire 1,250 year Jihad that is commonly known.

The term "blue blood" comes from the Moorish occupation of Spain. Spaniards have very white skin and the Moors were much darker. So the blue colored veins on the Spaniard's forearm were much more visible than the veins on a Moors' darker forearms. A 'blue blood' was a Spaniard, not a Moor.

The Jihad was finally, if only temporarily, stopped in France in 732. The Moorish army crossed over the Pyrenees Mountains from Spain into France, but waiting for them was Charles Martel and a hastily formed, but ferocious, army of Franks armed with war axes. They met at a city named Tours (or Poitiers) in western France, and after the great battle, Charles Martel was then known as Charles "The Hammer" Martel. It is not unreasonable to assume that he saved all of Europe from the heretofore unstoppable wave of the Jihad.

But by the end of these first 110 years of conquest, the Jihad had conquered from Spain to India, including the Middle East, N. Africa, and the Byzantine and Persian Empires. It was one of the largest and fastest conquests in world history. And they were not finished yet.

The campaign for Sicily lasted from 827 to 902 and the island was occupied for 264 years.

The Jihad arrived in St. Tropez on the French Riviera in 898 when a boat carrying 20 Moors was blown off course. The entire area was largely unguarded and even this small band was able to massacre entire towns. Word that they had discovered the most delightful place on earth soon spread and other Moors swelled the invading ranks. They murdered and plundered their way across southern France to Northern Italy and up into Switzerland. They "slaughtered the Christians in such numbers that a book published in Turin described one place where the Christians died as 'the Field of Martyrs'".44 They found the Alps mountain passes particularly suited to their trade and "'The number of Christians they killed is so great that only he who has written their names in the Book of Life can know of the number' wrote Liutprand'"45 The area was occupied for

---

44 Jihad in the West, ibid, pg. 136
45 ibid, pg. 138

only 75 years, partly because many of the invaders discovered that the French Riviera was better than Allah and decided to stay, convert and intermarry.

Constantinople was the next big prize and many battles, with many dramatic stories with each one, accompany its long defense and final capitulation in 1453. Its defenders were favored with some great commanders and with the dreaded "Greek Fire", both of which added to the drama. But it is now Istanbul.

Some of the nations that converted to Islam became some of its most successful warriors. Turkey is a good example. Turkey was the scene of many of St. Paul's missionary trips and was a Christian nation. After its conquest, this same nation supplied the Muslim armies that invaded and occupied Eastern Europe and the Balkan States and became the center of the Ottoman Turkish Empire.

The Moors that invaded and occupied Spain were N. African converts. The Mongols that invaded and occupied Russia for 240 years (1240-1480) were Mongolian converts. The Mongol version of Islam was very strict and severe. They went about executing Russians who professed Christianity with religious determination, but they found the numbers so great and the country so large that they stopped trying after a few dozen million.

The last 500 years of conquest was aimed at Eastern Europe. There were hundreds of battles and countless atrocities. Bosnia and Chechnya plague us today as a result. Hungary's war, occupation and resistance were a horror the Hungarians will never forget or recover from.

Muslims occupied Spain for 777 years, Portugal for 600 years, Greece 500 years, Bulgaria 500 years, Serbia 400 years, Rumania 400 years, Russia 240 years, and Hungary for 150 years.

In addition to their land campaigns, the Barbary pirates raided England, Denmark, Ireland and Iceland to seize people whom they sold into slavery.

I have some knowledge of military history, so let me share a little insight. Every time that I say there was a battle, you need to understand that every battle included thousands, or perhaps hundreds of thousands, of families that sent their fathers, sons and husbands off to war. The swords were sharpened, the often lazy and incompetent commanders threw aside sound military strategy, trenches were dug, horses were groomed and spies were sent out. Fortifications were prepared, hasty alliances were sought but rarely secured, sleepless nights were spent in prayer and wild guesses were made as to the enemy's strength. Buddies shared desperate hopes and dreams, screaming armies charged each other, arrows flew, horses ran into spears, scimitars swung, blood flowed. Thousands of men died and the survivors wrenched from the stench of disemboweled bodies left on the battlefield. All of this devastation was done in the name of Allah the Merciful.

Each campaign and each battle had its own

personal list of horrors. One of the most horrific was the Mongol Timurlane, the Muslim ruler of Samarkand. In the Georgian region of the Caucasus, he destroyed 700 towns and villages and killed thousands of Christians because the Georgian prince was too slow coming to Timurlane when called. In Silvas (Asia Minor), in 1402, Timurlane buried 4,000 Christian Armenians alive, but only after tying their bodies in a particularly painful position.[46]

It is a common belief that all conquered nations were given the choice between becoming Muslim or becoming dead. This is not altogether true. After the customary beheading of the losing army, the abduction of all the pretty girls and the sale of all marketable people into slavery, the occupying Muslims were much more interested in money and humiliating people than forcing conversions. It is true that any who openly confessed Jesus as Lord was summarily executed, but a sword was not put to every throat demanding conversion. Non-Muslims were forced to pay a large tax and were subjected to continual cruelty and humiliation. They could not wear shoes or ride a horse. They could not wear green, the color of Islam, or fight back if struck by a Muslim. It was much more fun to have tax-paying whipping boys around than more Muslims. Still, since this social pressure was so intense, and showed no signs of abating, it was only natural that most people

---

46 <u>Jihad in the West</u>, Paul Fregosi, pg. 238

eventually converted. But there really can be no doubt; the Jihad was more about money, slaves, power and young women than it was about Allah.

Also, if you have Gabriel as accessible as Muhammad did, then you can sweeten the pot even more. According to Muhammad, if a Muslim died in a Jihad, he did not have to wait to enter paradise like the other Muslims did. He is ushered into paradise immediately. Once in paradise, the martyr is given 72 "houris" for his continual sexual pleasure. Each houris is as lovely as rubies, as beautiful as coral, and with the complexion of diamonds and pearls. Each one is a virgin and her virginity is renewable. They have sex continually, lying on silk couches with green cushions and beautiful carpets. Their orgasms last 1,000 years and are intensified 100 times more than normal. Also, each martyr has 300 servants in paradise. Every day, each servant brings him a meal on a golden plate. That makes 300 sumptuous meals a day.[47] Nothing is said about women.

All this adds up to a lot of very inspired soldiers in the Muslim army. If they lived through the battle, they would be rich and have lots of beautiful girls as their sex slaves. If they died, they would spend eternity having sex with 72 gorgeous virgins. Either way, they won. These amazing rewards not only inspired the troops, it encouraged new converts. For the poor desert people, it

---

[47] (entire paragraph) Jihad in the West, Paul Fregosi, pg. 66

was nothing short of irresistible. Before each battle, the commanders would shout, "The houris are waiting for you!!"[48] Not even Napoleon could motivate his troops like that.

Centuries before, the Roman Empire began to struggle financially when its period of expansion slowed down and eventually stopped. It had plenty of money when it plundered new territories, but when that stopped and a series of civil wars started, the money really dried up. The same can be said of the Muslim empire. Times were great as long as there was plenty of loot, slaves and pretty young women flowing into the system, but when expansion stopped, that stopped too. Then the Muslim world settled down into a life of harsh autocratic rulers, poverty, backgammon, belly dancers, toothless fat wives, strong coffee, and tales of past glory.

---

48 ibid, pg. 68

Chapter 5
Islam and Women

There are 1.6 billion Muslims on earth today (2012), accounting for 23% of the world's population. That means there are 800 million Muslim women on earth today comprising 11.5% of the world's population. Would it matter to you if they comprise the single most oppressed people group on earth today? By oppressed, I mean they belong, in every sense of the word, to their husband or father. In strict Muslim countries, they enjoy no civil or human rights, independence, or freedom of thought or action. They exist to serve their man, and their lives and their enjoyment of life are subject to his whim and fancy, which is traditionally brutal. The word "Islam" means "submission", and the Muslim culture takes it both literally and seriously.

If Western feminist activists want to pursue a just cause, let it be this. The injustice that one Muslim woman endures in a single day exceeds all the gender injustice that the single most oppressed Western woman endures in a lifetime. And you can multiply that by 800 million.

A Muslim woman has put her life on the line and written a book exposing the plight of Muslim women. It is <u>A God Who Hates, the courageous woman who inflamed the Muslim world speaks out against the evils of Islam</u> by Wafa Sultan. 49 She has ignored the threats and intimidation

---

49 <u>A God Who Hates, the courageous woman who inflamed the Muslim</u>

that suppressed other Muslim women and told their story in brutal detail. She vividly portrays the oppression subjected on Muslim women by their mullahs, muftis and culture. She sets forth the tenets of her faith that explicitly deprive women of all rights and empower men to do with them whatever they want, including murder and castration. She also reveals how the culture has developed a social pattern of continual disagreement and a form of conversation that consists entirely of shrieking and screaming rather than a normal two-way exchange.[50]

She makes a convincing case that the "hate-filled and vengeful god"[51] of the Muslim religion hates women.

---

world speaks out against the evils of Islam, by Wafa Sultan, 2009, St. Martin's Press, 175 Fifth Ave., NY, NY 10010
50 ibid pages 4-6
51 ibid page 8

Chapter 6
Psychological Profile of Muhammad

Up to this point, I have restricted this book to historical facts, interspersed with what I consider to be only the most obvious of observations. I will now stray from that restriction and offer my layman's assessment of the man Muhammad and his religion. I am not a psychologist, but I am as much a student of human nature as the next man and believe that the conclusions that I draw are nothing more than any objective person would draw who had the facts before him as I do.

If the Qur'an was not dictated to Muhammad by Gabriel, then it came from Muhammad's own mind and the writing should reflect the man's personal knowledge, experiences, feelings, attitudes, desires and everything else that went into his psyche. So let's compare Muhammad's life before he met Gabriel to his life after that, and see if the psychological profile fits.

Muhammad's father died before he was born, so he grew up without the benefit of a father's love, discipline, guidance, training, support, protection or role model. Then, on two separate occasions, he experienced his own mother's rejection when she refused to care for him and forced him onto a Bedouin nurse for his first five years of life. This routinely causes people to feel rejected, insecure, resentful, rebellious and bitter. They often exhibit either extreme shyness or an extreme lack of discipline. They almost always have identity problems, self esteem problems and instability. It is commonly said they have a "chip on their shoulder".

As a young child, Muhammad reported a strange visitation where two men in white apparel opened up his stomach and looked around. He may have done this just to get attention because he felt unwanted, but those around him considered it very strange behavior.

When he was six and in the middle of the Arabian Desert, he watched his mother die before his eyes and leave him stranded in the middle of the desert with only a slave girl. This level of trauma is so extreme that one could rightfully say, "Unless you have experienced this yourself, you can have no idea what it is like". Now add to that the fact that now, he was an orphan.

It should come as no surprise that as a youth, Muhammad got into a lot of fights and acquired several bitter enemies. Remember the boy he kicked in the balls. Muhammad was a rough and ruthless loner.

It was only going to get worse. At age eight, disappointment reached an all time high when his beloved and indulgent grandfather died and all semblance of family and clan security disappeared.

Almost everyone struggles with the issues of identity and self-esteem at some point in their lives. These struggles can be very difficult under the best of circumstances. With orphans without adoptive parents, it seems to be more difficult than with most. Particularly during the teen years, when peer pressures are strongest and personal identity and status are so important, it is invaluable to have parents around to offer encouragement and guidance. Muhammad lost his father before he was born, then his mother and then his grandfather. He was an orphan and very much alone. His conflicts with the leaders of his tribe attest to the fact that this orphan was not dealing well with normal growth issues and social pressures. It is only natural that a poor orphan would be wild and rough and not well behaved or personally secure. Add to this the problems of being considered low class by the Christians and Jews around him, the overcrowded conditions and the general lawlessness of the time and place, and you do not have an average middle class upbringing. Muhammad had all the ingredients for wild behavior and instability. He apparently grew into manhood without ever resolving these issues or attaining stability within himself or with his clan.

Twice in my life I have had the occasion to work on projects involving men who have been less fortunate than most. One involved visiting and working with inmates at a prison. I soon began to notice how many of the inmates did not have fathers. So I looked into it and learned that 75% of all male inmates in prisons and jails grew up without a father in their home. And these men grew up in modern America, not 6th Century Arabia.

The other project involved working with poor men in the inner city. They were not criminals, just poor, but again I noticed the same thing. In almost every case, they had grown up without a father in their house. These men had the same insecurity as the prisoners, but rather than becoming aggressive and belligerent, these men had become defeatists. They lacked confidence.

As I have already said, Arabia was poor, wild and lawless and the fierce desert tribes fought continually. This led Muhammad to believe that the different tribes should unite and stop the self-destruction. He also learned the benefits of robbing caravans.

Muhammad's work history shows a serious dislike for real work. He was 25 before he got his first job and then only because his uncle threw him out. Then he quickly married his boss for her money, even though she was 15 years older.

He was an Arab in a world of Arabs, Christians and Jews, and the Arabs were at the bottom looking up. He experienced prejudice and even hatred up close and personal.

The Christians and Jews lived a much higher lifestyle and even before meeting Gabriel, Muhammad was outspoken in his belief that the Arabs' problems were partly religious. He believed that there was only one God and the Arabs' polytheism and idolatry was utter foolishness. He paid rapt attention to the teachers at the Ocatz Fair and picked up some of the basic points; such as Abraham, Isaac, Jacob, Ishmael, the chosen people, Moses, Jesus, Gabriel and tithing.

During his first marriage, he was to suffer the loss of five of his six children. The death of one's child is considered the worst tragedy that anyone can suffer and the event that causes the deepest grief humanly possible. He went through this experience five times.

Even men who have lived a stable life still go through a crisis of purpose around the age of 40. As everyone knows, it is called "mid-life crisis" and is very real. Muhammad's encounter with Gabriel occurred when he was 40 years old.

That is my summary of the relevant events in his life before Gabriel, and it is certainly plenty of material for this amateur psychologist to work with.

Now to compare the man Muhammad before age 40 with the religion he started and his behavior as its prophet.

As previously pointed out, all of the initial tenets of his new religion were the same as his personal beliefs before Gabriel. One doesn't need a PhD in psychology to recognize the significance of that.

Islam places Ishmael as the heir of the promises of God to Abraham, and thus made the Arabs God's chosen race.[52] This stroke of genius could easily be the result of his own personal conclusions combined with the kind of extravagant zeal and desperation that his desperate conditions created within him. By this simple "end run", he bettered both the hated Christians and Jews. It was very sweet and simple. In the same brilliant stroke, he raised a standard around which all Arabs could rally, and

---

[52] Qur'an 2:122, 2:127

gave them identity, status and a very high calling. Who is to say he did not simply make it up?

After his power base was secure, the social reforming and moral crusading Muhammad disappeared and the military conqueror appeared. The new religion had a totally new face. The real Muhammad had emerged and this is the Muhammad of history. The conquest was on! Much of the world would feel the sting of the Muslim sword and correcting the wrongs to orphans and girl babies had nothing to do with it. It was now all about treasure and young women.

One of Muhammad's first acts as Prophet-turned-Commander was to torture a local Jew to learn where he kept his treasure, then to kill 700 Jews for no reason. This behavior is more consistent with Muhammad's temperament and character before becoming prophet than with the tenets of any religion.

Muhammad made it a law that he and the ruling caliphs after him were to receive one-fifth of all treasure taken in conquests. He had to better the Jewish tithe. He doubled it.

Muhammad did not have a single girlfriend until he got married, but he was to make up for lost time. He had eleven wives plus concubines.[53] Some accounts

---

[53]

1. Khadijah, age 55, in 595, died 619. They had 6-7 children. Only Fatimah survived.
2. Sawda, age 35-40, from Abyssinia in 620, two

months after Khadijah died.

  3. A'isha, age 6, in 620, daughter of Abu Bakr, was Muhammad's undisputed favorite wife.

  4. Hafsa, age 18, in Feb. 625, Umar's daughter.

  5. Zainab, in Mar. 625, widow of Muhammad's cousin Ubaidah, killed in the Battle of Badr. She died 3-8 months later. Permission to exceed the Qur'an's limit of four wives is granted in Qur'an 33:50.

  6. Salama, age under 29, in 626, widow. A'isha was jealous of her.

  7. Zainab bint Jahsh, age almost 40, in June 626, the divorced wife of Muhammad's adopted son Zaid. Referenced in Qur'an 33:37.

  8. Juwairiya, in Dec.626-Jan. 627, captured in raid on Bani Mastalik after the Battle of the Trench. Widow of defeated chief. When wife #3, A'isha, first saw Juwairiya, she said, "When I saw her... I was filled with misgivings, for I knew the Prophet would see in her what I saw, her great loveliness and beauty."

  9. Umm Habiba, in 627-628, given to Muhammad in marriage by the Negus. She was the daughter of Abu Sufyan, Muhammad's arch enemy. Her brother, Mu'awiyah, became caliph and Ali's rival for caliph.

  10. Safiyah, age 17, in 628, widow of murdered Jewish chief after slaughter at Khaibar. She was very beautiful.

  11. Maimunah, age 51, in 629-630, the widow of a relative.

Concubines: Mary the Copt (Christian) and Rihana (Jew). One account says he married Mary. Muslims were tolerant of concubines because the father of their race, Ishmael, was number his wives at 21. The Qur'an gave Muhammad the right to marry as many as he wished, *(4:24)* forbade that any wife remarry and required that "when you ask his wives anything, ask only from behind a curtain." *(33:53)* The Qur'an allowed polygamy and the Islamic society that emerged was almost built around the pleasures of a harem. One of Muhammad's wives, Aisha, was only six years old when he married her, but he did wait until she was nine before he consummated the marriage.

The changes in Muhammad's life are also readily evident in the Qur'an. When he was in the recruitment phase, he was the social reformer. After his position was secure, his emphasis turned to bringing every area of Arab life under his personal authority. He empowered himself with all authority to decide all disputes whether civil, criminal or religious. He designated himself as the last of the prophets, elevating himself to the level of final authority for all times throughout the universe. *(Qur'an 33:40)*

---

the child of Abraham's concubine of a sort (his wife's maid).

Muhammad was not the least bit shy about granting himself authority or showering himself with praise. According to Muhammad, God told Muhammad that Muhammad was: favored by God[54], a beautiful pattern of conduct[55], the one to believe in[56], has an exalted standard of character[57], deserving of honor[58], is judge[59], is not severe or harsh hearted[60], is the messenger of Allah[61], nearest of kin to Abraham[62], that all others must obey him[63], sanctifies the people[64], sent by Allah

---

[54] Qur'an 9:117, 48:2, 68:2, 93:3-8, 94:1, 108:1

[55] 33:21

[56] 4:136, 170; 7:158; 13:43; 24:62; 46:31; 48:9, 13; 49:15; 57:7, 28; 58:4; 61:11; 64:8

[57] 68:4

[58] 63:8; 69:40

[59] 4:59,65, 83, 105; 5:48; 24:51; 42:15

[60] 3:159

[61] 33:40; 48:28-29; 49:7; 63:1

[62] 3:68

[63] 3:32; 4:59, 64, 69; 5:92; 8:1, 20-21, 46; 9:71; 24:51-54, 56; 33:33, 36; 33:71; 47:33; 48:16-17; 49:14; 58:13; 60:12; 64:12

[64] 62:2

with guidance and the religion of truth[65], must be spoken to with respect[66], is wise[67] and the universal Messenger[68]. Again, Muhammad said that God said all this to Muhammad about Muhammad. No other person was involved in this process.

Gabriel came in handy whenever Muhammad got hot pants. Once Muhammad saw the wife of his adopted son Zeid half dressed and exclaimed, "Gracious Lord, Good heavens! How dost thou turn the hearts of men."[69] She got the message and repeated the story to her hideous husband, who became terrified and promptly divorced her. In the meantime, Gabriel appeared to Muhammad and told him that it was God's will that he marry his daughter-in-law.[70] Still, there was some gossip about Muhammad marrying his daughter-in-law, so Gabriel appeared again and told Muhammad, "Oh prophet, why hast thou forbidden thyself that which God hath made lawful to thee, seeking the good pleasures of thy wives? ... God has ordained for you the absolution of

---

[65] 61:9

[66] 2:104; 4:46; 24:62; 33:56-57; 49:1-5; 58:8

[67] 62:2

[68] 34:28

69 Jihad in the West, Paul Fregosi, pg. 49
[70] Qur'an, Sura 33

your oaths... God is your protector."[71] Muhammad must obey Allah. The total sexual freedom that Muhammad wanted was exactly what he gave to himself and to his religion.

The Jihad and the Islamic society profited greatly from slavery, and both the leaders and warriors enjoyed the benefits and pleasures of many slaves, particularly pretty young women. This darker side of Islam and its Jihad is consistent with the bitterness, prejudice and inhumanity suffered by Muhammad while growing up and again very difficult to reconcile with the tenets of any religion.

By far the most conspicuous feature of Muhammad's behavior as prophet, the Qur'an and the 1,250 year Jihad was the call to kill all infidels and the savage butchery that ensued as they carried out these commands. No other culture can rival the death toll that they chalked up.[72] Islam's total disregard for the value of human life is unrivaled in human history and Islam demands that the target of this attack, which is the rest of humanity, accept their death sentence as the will of God.

Consider the influences that must have boiled in Muhammad's heart and soul to produce such an attitude

---

[71] Qur'an, Sura 66

72 Mao Tse Tung reportedly killed 70 million Chinese in his cultural revolution and Hitler killed somewhere between 40 and 50 million in WWII. That was in the middle of the 20th Century when the world's population was 3 billion. During the time of the Jihad, the world's

toward the rest of mankind:
born without a father
rejected by his mother at birth
again rejected by his mother at age two
rejected a third time by his mother at age four
watched his mother die at age six
left alone in the middle of the desert with a slave at age six
suffered the tragic loss of his indulgent grandfather at age eight
lived the life of a very poor orphan
strongly disliked by the chief of his tribe
considered a coward by his peers
asked to leave home at age 25, and
suffered the tragic death of five of six children.

To all these natural disasters, we add a reclusive and antagonistic temperament and the end result is a plan for an all-out assault on humanity.

Human nature is fragile. Each of us has both a heart and a soul, and each can be deeply affected by tragedy. I have met many people who struggle their whole lives with a single traumatic childhood event. Some are unable to ever recover from the hurt. Any one of the traumatic events in Muhammad's life could be characterized as tragic enough to severely hamper normal development, and he had a dozen. And in his

---

population was only ½ billion, and it killed untold millions.

case, he suffered the most tragic event of all, the death of one's small child, five times.

Remember the time Muhammad watched for ten to twelve hours as one by one, 700 Jews were beheaded before him. I know a woman who took an anatomy class in medical school and one day the class had to dissect a head. She said that when the head was uncovered, they saw that the head had been severed from the body. The whole class gagged, reeled back and voiced their horror. She said that this event was one of the most stressful and traumatic events in her life. She said that when you look at a head that has been detached from the body, it is very different than looking at a severed hand or foot. It is the single most dehumanizing thing she could imagine. Now imagine the kind of man that would enjoy watching closely as a man is dragged in front of him, the man is shoved down, a scimitar is swung across his neck, his head falls to the ground with a thud and blood spurts out of the stump between his shoulders. And watching this 700 times in a single day! This trait is more consistent with a man of Muhammad's background than with the doctrine of a religion, any religion, dictated by an angel of the one true God.

All in all, in my layman's opinion, the Qur'an fits Muhammad's psychological profile perfectly. The Qur'an that was dictated by Muhammad, and Muhammad's behavior as prophet, and the traditions that he started and were followed for 13 centuries, are all consistent with the psychological profile of Muhammad the man. In every respect, Muhammad created what he personally wanted.

All other world religions share certain common characteristics. Most basic with all other religions is the belief that man can achieve some degree of acceptance by God through God's grace or man's good works. In each case, the religion requires that people try to be good. However, this is not the case with Islam, where they are commanded to kill all infidels, which are all non-Muslims. It is the only "religion" of its kind in the world.

Bibliography

Jihad in the West, Muslim Conquests from the 7th to the 21st Centuries, by Paul Fregosi, Premetheus Books, 1998

Life of Mohomet, by Sir William Muir, K.C.S.I., Smith, Elder & Co., 1894

Muhammad the Messenger of God, by Betty Kelen, Thomas Nelson, Inc. 1975

The New Encyclopedia Britannica, 15th Edition, "Muhammad"

World Book Encyclopedia, 1993, "Muhammad"

The Encyclopedia Americana, International Edition, Grolier Incorporated, "Muhammad"

The Qur'an Translation, translated by M.H. Shakir, published by Tahrike Tarsile Qur'an, Inc., 80-08 51st Avenue, Elmhurst, New York 11373, 14th U.S. Ed., 2003

Islam Unveiled, by Robert Spencer, Encounter Books, San Francisco, 2002

Muslims, their religious beliefs and practices, by Andrew Rippin, 1990, published by Routledge, 270 Madison Ave., NY, NY 10016

A God Who Hates, the courageous woman who inflamed the Muslim world speaks out against the evils of Islam, by Wafa Sultan, 2009, St., Martin's Press, 175 Fifth Ave., NY, NY 10010

www.ingramcontent.com/pod-product-compliance
Lightning Source LLC
Chambersburg PA
CBHW060704030426
42337CB00017B/2753